My Comedy Calendar

Sketches for Two

Kim Wedler

TSL Drama

Contents

January in 'The Black Forest'

Anna has been walking in The Black Forest, she has fallen down a hole. A big hole. It is now getting dark, and she suddenly has a signal on her phone. She randomly dials, as she does not know the number for the emergency services to get her out. She is not hurt, just a bit embarrassed and cold.

Voice on phone: Guten Tag! Hansel and Pretzel. Das Willkommen, Ich heiße Helga!

Anna: Oh... Hi do you spekondi English?

Helga: Ja, a little.

Anna: My name is Anna and I am stuck down a hole.

Helga: Ja. [*pause*]

Anna: I need help, could you phone the fire brigade. [*silence*]

The... er... [*makes the sound of a fire engine*]

Helga: Ja. Feuerwehrauto. [*pause*] Nine.

Anna: No, I only need one.

Helga: Nine, I mean... No, we had feuerwehrauto out last week for strudel fire! Sorry, this line is only for customers, Auf Wiedersehen.

Anna: No, no don't hang up! Ok, does the strudel come warm, with ice cream?

Helga: Ja.

Anna: Ok. I'll have one of those.

Helga: Eat in or take away?

Anna: Listen, if I order the strudel can you deliver it, in a big truck by a big strong man, with ropes?

Helga:	A big truck? For one strudel? There will be a lot of room in truck.
Anna:	Ok... What else do you do?
Helga:	We do Berliner.
Anna:	What's that?
Helga:	It is round and fried pastry with jam in the middle.
Anna:	You mean a doughnut!
Helga:	Ja, it is the German cousin of the doughnut!
Anna:	Ok, I'll have two of those. I'll also have... What do you people call it? Taken, nicked!
Helga:	The nicked?
Anna:	Yes, it's got a name that is like, when you take something that doesn't belong to them. Nicked, taken, stolen.
Helga:	Oh, stolen, the stollen cake, yes... We also have Schneeballen.
Anna:	Bless you!
Helga:	No, schneeballen is a German speciality, it consists of thin strips of shortcrust pastry that are loosely intertwined and wrapped into balls which are deep-fried until golden and crispy.
Anna:	Yes, gold, and crispy.
Helga:	Traditional versions are dusted with sugar, but there are also variations may be covered in chocolate glaze or different combinations of nuts, coconut, cinnamon, or marzipan.
Anna:	Great, what do they come in?
Helga:	A box.
Anna:	How many in a box?
Helga:	A box of 12.
Anna:	Great, I'll have six of those!!

Helga:	Six!! That is a lot of food for one person!
Anna:	Yes, but can you send a truck now?
Helga:	A truck?
Anna:	A van, can you send van?
Helga:	Yes. Van. We have also a special on Bratwurst, Blutwurst and Schwarzwurst buy five – get the six free.
Anna:	Wonderful, those as well.
Helga:	Gift wrapped?
Anna:	No, that's fine.
Helga:	Red bows?
Anna:	If you like.
Helga:	Okey-dokey, shall I read you back your order?
Anna:	No!!
Helga:	Ok, 55 Euros.
Anna:	55 Euros!!!??
Helga:	You want the order or not!!
Anna:	Yes, sorry.
Helga:	Address...
Anna:	The Hole, Black Forest, Germany.
Helga:	What number, 'The Hole'?
Anna:	[agitated] Can you possibly just track my phone?
Helga:	Ja.
Anna:	Good, ooh and a coffee please, with milk and sugar.
Helga:	Ok, so we have a Berliner, a stollen, six boxes of Schneeballen, a...
Anna:	I'll pay 60 Euros when he gets here.
Helga:	Very good. Cash or Card?
Anna:	Card.

Helga:	Debit or credit.
Anna:	Debit!!
Helga:	Ich heiße Helga, Hansel, and Pretzel. Das Willkommen. Auf Wiedersehen.
	[*20 minutes later, bright lights are seen*]
Anna:	Oh, thank goodness, over here!! No down here!! Yoo hoo. I need help.
	That isn't a truck, it's a moped! I asked for a van.
Teenage girl:	Ja, I am Van, Vanessa, you asked for me!!
Anna:	No, I wanted a van with ropes to pull me out.
Teenage girl:	Ja, I am Van, I have ropes!!
Anna:	Oh, ok.
Teenage girl:	That is 60 Euros.
Anna:	[*moves phone over*] There is an app on my phone.
Teenage girl:	You have lastest iphone it is good ja? I cannot afford new iphone on my money. [*hands her an enormous bag of food and a coffee*]. I tie rope on bag, and other end on big tree.
	[*Teenage girl leaves as Anna slurps the coffee*]
Anna:	Hey, where are you going? That's my phone!!! I don't believe it... [*pause*] Not even any sugar in this coffee.

My funny valentine

A couple, who didn't think they would ever find love, talk about their relationship. They are recording it for a reality show.

Rachel: So, I'm Rachel.

Neville: I'm Neville.

Rachel: We met using on-line dating. 'Quirky.dot.com'.

Neville: I liked Rachel straight away, she had kind eyes and a nice blue jumper with shiny buttons.

Rachel: I liked Neville, he had nice glasses and a fun tie.

Neville: I had on my train tie, as I love trains.

Rachel: Our first date was at Watford Park, to see the steam train. Neville had looked it up online. We didn't know until we got there that it was a miniature railway. It was ok, I was happy going around with my knees touching my elbows. Neville was so happy, waving his handkerchief like a little flag. We stopped for an ice cream, didn't we?

Neville: Yes, I'd brought a cool box with me. It had Cornettos in it. The cool box was new. The Cornettos weren't, they were from my freezer, from home.

Rachel: He'd emptied his penny jar to buy the cool box. He loves collecting things. He collects pennies.

Neville: And jars.

Rachel: Oh yes, remember what we said to each other on-line?

Neville: Oh, yes, that I collect coloured jars and you said...

Rachel: And I said, I make jam... to put in his jars. It was fate!!

Neville: So, after the Cornettos I folded up my cool bag and put it in my cagoule. It has lots of useful pockets.

Rachel: After the Cornettos we went for a long walk along the canal. Neville knows everything about canals.

Neville: Canals are formed by piling dirt, stone, concrete, or other building materials. The finished shape of the canal is known as the canal prism.

Rachel: A few ducks splashed as we walked by, they made you jump didn't they Neville?

Neville: Yes, not a fan of flying creatures.

Rachel: You wore a lovely jumper with a train on it, didn't you? Neville doesn't usually wear jumpers; he prefers tank tops.

Neville: I don't really like jumpers, too constricting and itchy.

Rachel: He wore a new jumper for one of our dates, didn't you? It was a paisley jumper. I knew it was new.

Neville: Yes, because I haven't cut the tag out.

Rachel: No, because you still had the coat hanger in the back of it.

Neville: I don't know how I did that! I usually put my coat hangers in my coat hanger collection.

Rachel: He loves collecting things.

Neville: Stamps, coloured jars, thimbles and buttons.

Rachel: Oh yes, your button collection.

Neville: Yes, I have over 600 of them.

Rachel: He loves buttons. [*pause*] He liked the buttons on my blue jumper on our first date. So, after the walk on our first date, Neville walked me to the bus garage to get my bus. He was going to get on with me, but he'd managed to get his cagoule stuck in the door of the bus in front and had to gallop alongside it to Rickmansworth. Good job, I hadn't got the train! [*pause*] It was a lovely day.

Neville: On our second date, I showed Rachel my curly whirly.

Rachel: He was so proud of it. On our third date, I got a glimpse of his walnut whip!

Neville: I collect them.

Rachel: Sweet wrappers.

Neville: Particularly, I like collecting 'Quality Street'. The sweets are free from artificial colours, flavourings and preservatives, and since 2009, the packaging has been completely recyclable. The coloured wrappers are compostable, while the foil wrappers and the tin container can be recycled in the same way as cans.

Rachel: Neville is so clever, he made me a fascinator out of the 'big purple one' wrappers.

Neville: Not all the supermarkets stock those ones. Quality Street is a selection of individual tinned or boxed toffees, chocolates and sweets, first manufactured by Mackintosh's in Halifax, West Yorkshire, England, in 1936. It was named after J. M. Barrie's play, Quality Street.

Rachel: He knows everything about them!

Neville: Yes, I do.

Rachel: So, here we are 10 months later, still happy and because we met last April, it's our first Valentine's day!

Neville: Actually Rachel, I have something to ask you.

Rachel: Yes Neville.

[Neville *produces a small jewellery box*]

Rachel: It isn't?

Neville: It is... Will you...?

Rachel: [*opens the box and screams with delight*] OOOHH!!

Neville: Will you be... the owner of my most prized button?

Rachel: I will. Oh, you really do love me, don't you Neville.

March into a play!

Sharon and Mary are sitting on small chairs, in a nursery setting. They have a child each, toddlers, called Johnny and Ronnie.

Mary: Ronnie, please don't put that in your mouth darling. That's it, make something out of the playdough. Yes, use the plastic knife. No, Ronnie not in your mouth, get it out of your mouth Ronnie.

Sharon: Johnny, you need to share with Ronnie.

Mary: No Ronnie, not in your mouth, get it out of your mouth, Ronnie. Ronnie takes Johnny's arm out of your mouth, Ronnie. Sorry Sharon, he didn't have his breakfast this morning.

Sharon: That's alright, always a bit of a rush in the morning, isn't it? I found a Werther's Original in my hair this morning. I wouldn't mind, but I don't buy them myself. Had a good week?

Mary: Yes, Peter finally erected the garden fence, his mother came over for lunch. We had an assortment of hors d'oeuvres and petit fours, I also managed to finish my book by Chimamanda Ngozi Adichie. How about you?

Sharon:	Well, thankfully my mother-in-law lives in Edinburgh. The most I've read this week is half a page of *Heat* magazine, which was at the dentist, and Martin hasn't had anything erect since last September. Oh, I have got some news though...
Mary:	Oh yes, go on.
Sharon:	I joined the local Am Dram group.
Mary:	You didn't...
Sharon:	I did...
Mary:	Ronnie please don't lick her; you don't know where she's been.
Sharon:	So, I turned up last Friday. They were not really my type of people.
Mary:	What, you mean a large group of 'thespians?
Sharon:	I don't know about that, one woman had halitosis, another had a wonky eye and I think she brushed up against my boob on purpose, so... maybe.
	Johnny... She doesn't want it in her hair, take it out.
Mary:	Why weren't they your type? You mean a bit 'full of themselves and arty.'
Sharon:	No, just looked like they'd all washed and combed their hair. Can't remember when I last did that.
Mary:	Ronnie take your finger out of your nose!! No Ronnie not in your mouth, get it out of your mouth, Ronnie.
Sharon:	Do you know last Wednesday. I went out with my top on back to front and inside out. I only noticed when I had my spaghetti that evening and dropped my bolognaise on the label. Marks and Spencer's... Marks and Spencer's, it said on the label, when have I ever been to Marks and Spencer's?
Mary:	I go there all the time. I use their hand lotion. Exquisite.

Sharon:	I use their car park. Discount City is in the high street. Anyway, you won't believe it. I got a part in their next production.
Mary:	Ronnie, put her down!!! What's it called?
Sharon:	What, the kid he's picked up? I don't know, some sort of herb, I think. Dill, Parsley. Oh, I know Paisley.
Mary:	No, not the child. The play.
Sharon:	It's called 'In bed with your idol' by Alan As-been. It's all about this woman called Susan, who dreams of meeting her idol.
Mary:	So, you play Susan?
Sharon:	No, I play the lollipop lady.
Mary:	The lollipop lady?
Sharon:	Yes, she has one of her 'dreams' while she's taking her kid to school.
	It was going to be played by some old bloke in the society, but his piles were playing him up, so he had to pull out... Out of the play that is.
Mary:	So... starting at the bottom, then.
Sharon:	Piles generally do.
Mary:	No, I meant your newfound acting career, starting at the bottom.
Sharon:	Oh yes, I see what you mean.
Mary:	This time next year everyone will be asking to see your 'Bottom'!
Sharon:	See my bottom?
Mary:	Shakespeare.
Sharon:	I'm not showing him my bottom – whoever he is.
Mary:	No, never mind, carry on.
Sharon:	So luckily, due to the senior's piles. I got the part on the spot. Beryl, the costume lady is going to take in the uniform and now I play 'Martine' instead of Martin.

Mary:	Well done you.
Sharon:	So, can I give you a leaflet? Do you think I can give them out to the mums?
Mary:	[*takes the leaflet, peering at it*] Oh dear. I'm so sorry Sharon you can't give out these leaflets.
Sharon:	Why's that?
Mary:	The BEDROOM bit, could be something a bit 'risqué.' She's lying on a bed.
Sharon:	Well, yes that's what people do when they go to bed.
Mary:	She has her night wear on.
Sharon:	It's flannelette pajamas, with Cherry Bakewell's on them.
Mary:	Oh, those are cherries. Ronnie, mouth... out...
	Also, Hampton Players.
Sharon:	Most groups are called players, on account of them playing parts.
Mary:	I'm sorry but this is a church nursery you know. It's not a group. I mean, what you do in your own time is up to you, so sorry.
Sharon:	Oh, I see, you don't like people having hobbies, is that it?
Mary:	Of course, that isn't it. As parishioners of this church, we have a reputation to maintain.
Sharon:	I'm not a parishioner of this church, they just do better biscuits than at the British Legion.
Mary:	Sharon, people are looking! We have to do the right thing!!
Sharon:	People are looking, you say!? Do the right thing? Is Ronnie doing the right thing? So far today he's put a marble, a piece of blu-tak and a small plastic duck in his mouth, not to mention my Johnny's arm. He's licked Rebecca and turned Parsley upside down until

she turned blue!!! Oh, and now he's got his hand down the back of his Calvin Kleins.

Mary: Well, I...

Sharon: And may I remind you, you were the one who mentioned somebody wanting to look at my backside!!

Mary: No, you've got it all wrong Sharon...

Sharon: It's a play Mary, the leaflet is for a family show. It doesn't say 'call Sharon for a good time'. Get your mind out of the gutter!!

[*motions to another mum*] Hiya Suzy, would you like a leaflet, I'm in a play. Oh! You would? Lovely.

Claudette? You're interested in joining? The next one? Oh yes, you can join for the next one. You'll love it. What are we doing? We're doing the 'Best little Whorehouse in Texas.'

Showers

Jackie enters the show room, she has been caught in the rain. She puts her umbrella in the stand and looks out of the window. She then nonchalantly looks at the shower units on offer, when she feels someone is behind her, she turns. The sales assistant is on top of her.

Derek: Hello, I'm Derek. Welcome to 'Showers are Us'. What type of shower can I help you with today?

Jackie: I'm just looking really, thank you.

Derek: No problem.

Jackie: Thanks.

Derek: Can I interest you in this little beauty. Power shower 101?

Jackie: Very nice thanks. Just looking.

Derek: On special this Easter weekend. 50% off!!

Jackie: Yes, very nice.

Derek: How much, you may ask? I can do you a special price, just for you!! I shouldn't do it, but I can see you are a lady that likes the finer things in life. I can see you have impeccable taste in clothes and have dined in the finest restaurants, am I right?

Jackie: [embarrassed but pleased] Well, yes. I do like nice things.

Derek: Between you and me, Victoria Beckham has this very shower in her house. I kid you not, imagine saying you have the same shower as her royal highness Victoria. Although to be honest, I can tell that you are much more classy!

Jackie: Well, I do try.

Derek:	Now, don't tell me... You have a special event coming up, don't you? A birthday, an anniversary, Easter?
Jackie:	Yes, I have my birthday coming up.
Derek:	Shouldn't your husband be treating you? What better way than a Beckham Power Shower 101.
Jackie:	I suppose.
Derek:	Of course, it's not only just for you. It's the present that keeps on giving! Got any kids?
Jackie:	Yes, a teenage boy.
Derek:	Bet he likes football.
Jackie:	Not really.
Derek:	Any hobbies?
Jackie:	Yes, he plays the cello.
Derek:	Big instrument that!! Lugging it around all day, what better than after practise... A power shower, the 101!
Jackie:	I suppose...
Derek:	What's your husband do... Construction?
Jackie:	No, he's an accountant.
Derek:	Even better. He would definitely know what a good investment this is!!!
	Can't put a price on cleanliness.
Jackie:	How much is it?
Derek:	Exactly!! Does your mum come around?
Jackie:	Yes, but not to use the shower.
Derek:	She will if you have the 101. I can promise you that!
Jackie:	I'll have to think about it.
Derek:	Remember the offer is only this weekend! Tell you what I'll also do, don't tell the boss. I will throw in a shower curtain. [opens a large book of designs] Got any hobbies?
Jackie:	I like baking!

Derek:	Brilliant, I've got ones with cupcakes on it. Look this one has this year's calendar on it.
Jackie:	Why would I want that?
Derek:	Your husband might, to reach his deadlines. This one has a mirrored finish, just to make sure you haven't missed any bits! Horses, pebbles, ducks. You name it; we've got it.
Jackie:	So, what would it cost me?
Derek:	Well, how much do you want to pay? Or a better question, when it comes to cleanliness how much is too much?
Jackie:	I don't really understand the question.
Derek:	Tell you what I'll do. I will send Dennis round to measure the bathroom and give an estimate with the fitting in costs. I'll book you in. I just need your name and address. We can do it on Thursday. Once we start the work it's pay up front. No refunds, no returns and we take no responsibility for the product.
Jackie:	Oh, I just remembered, I'm out on Thursday.
Derek:	Well, we are extremely busy, but I think we can squeeze you in Monday, Tuesday, Wednesday, or Friday.
Jackie:	Let me think about it and get back to you.
Derek:	Entirely up to you of course. But when it's gone it's gone. Don't want you disappointed or waking up in a sweat. Won't have that power shower to cool you off!
Jackie:	No, it's fine... I'll come back later.
Derek:	Alright, take my card. Maybe I can interest you in a new Shower Head. Shower Valve, Shower Cartridge, Shower Strainer, Shower Pan...

May Day celebrations

Doris resides in Merry Weathers care home. Her granddaughter has come to see her.

Lorraine: Hello Nana. How are you?

Nanna: Oh, hello, lovely. Did you remember my Garibaldi's, Jaffa cakes and tea?

Lorraine: Yes, bit of confusion about the Garibaldi's, the Saturday girl in the supermarket thought I was referring to the supervisor in soft furnishings.

Nanna: What about my aubergine?

Lorraine: Yes, although why you would need that, isn't the food good enough?

Nanna: Oh, it's not for eating. The aubergine and a few of my cordial bottles, makes a good indoor game of bowling.

[*Pause*]

How's your mum?

Lorraine: She's fine.

Nanna: How's that fella she's married to?

Lorraine: You mean my dad, he's fine.

Nanna: Still boring, is he? Speaking of dull, we had a party here last Friday.

Lorraine: That sounds nice.

Nanna: We had it for VD Day.

Lorraine: It's VE Day Nanna, not VD Day.

Nanna: Oh, so, I didn't need to tell them about that evening in the air raid shelter with the 'Carter triplets'? Anyway, talking of spread, we had a nice one for the celebrations.

Lorraine: That's nice to have a spread.

Nanna: Yes, it was that 'Primula' squeezy cheese with bits of ham.

Lorraine: Anything else?

Nanna: Few sausage rolls and jelly.

Lorraine: Did it bring back memories of the war?

Nanna: We were only allowed one quarter of a sandwich and a few crisps, so yes. It was similar to the rationing.

Lorraine: Well, at least you were all together.

Nanna: Friday, we had it! Friday!! 'Bank Holiday Friday' whose idea was that? We usually have fish on Friday, not sandwiches. Threw us all off. Winnie thought it was Sunday, thought she'd missed Friday and doubled up on her pills. Nearly died of an overdose. Still she looked quite happy when she came around to find 'Aaron' the new young carer giving her the kiss of life.

   [*pause*] Look at her. She's had that silly grin on her face all week.

Lorraine: Anyone share any interesting stories?

Nanna: Oh, yes, Bill said he had PTSD.

Lorraine: Really? That can be very upsetting.

Nanna: Yes, He told us what it stood for.

   [*at the same time*]

Lorraine: Post traumatic...

Nanna: Putting too much sugar in your drinks. Awful, and he's a diabetic!!

Lorraine: PTSD, stands for post-traumatic stress disorder.

Nanna: I get that, when I don't receive my bank statement. [*pause*]

   They keep telling me to do it online. I don't want to do it online. They want passwords, security questions. Mother's maiden name, I can't even remember my own name, let alone my mother's. Favourite pet, favourite colour!! No thank you.

Lorraine: So, what about after your food, what happened then?

Nanna: Stan got his harmonica out and played 'The white cliffs of Dover', very nice. Albert played the spoons.

Lorraine: That sounds lovely!

Nanna: Then we listened to Vera Glyn sing 'We'll meet again'.

Lorraine: It's Vera Lyn, Nanna.

Nanna: No, Vera Glyn, that's her over there in the pink cardy. She's got an alright voice, bit of a lovey though. Used to do amateur dramatics, she was doing voice exercises in the kitchen for half an hour before she made her entrance.

Lorraine: Well, I'm glad you had a nice time. [*pause*] It's just a flying visit I'm afraid this week. I've got to pack for Uni later today.

Nanna: Oh, yes who'd have thought it? My Granddaughter studying pornography.

Lorraine: It's photography, Nanna.

Nanna: Yeah, you get off love. I've got a game of poker to go to in an hour.

Lorraine: Poker? I really don't like the idea of you gambling.

Nanna: Don't worry, what do you think I wanted the Garibaldi's and Jaffa cakes for. [*pause*] Anyway, I seem to have a knack at winning. Last week I cleaned up, took all of Alan's Hob Nobs and 'Terry's chocolate orange'. He wasn't pleased! But that's the way the cookie crumbles, especially in this builders' tea! See ya love!!

Over the moon in June

Kevin and Elaine have been married for 10 years. She wanted Kevin to surprise her with a gift for their anniversary. She is not happy with his choice of surprise.

Kevin: Something different, you said, surprise me you said. I don't want the usual, you said. I don't want flowers and chocolates, you said. 10 years of marriage, you said.

Elaine: Yes, Kev, 10 years of marriage and you still haven't got a clue about what I want. You never listen, never did.

Kevin: I did listen my angel, you said you wanted something out of this world.

Elaine: Yes, I did.

Kevin: There you go!

Elaine: I also said, Kevin, look at those white stilettos in the shoe shop. Kevin, that bag in Debenhams would go lovely with those white stilettos. It's like the time I said, Kevin, I'd love a wonderful meal with some expensive wine. What did you get me? Not a meal out, but a slow cooker.

Kevin: Don't forget, I got the wine.

Elaine: From the petrol station, on the way home from work.

Kevin: Well, their wine is expensive! Out of this world you said, so that's what I got you.

Elaine: Why would you think that meant a week at the Kennedy Space Camp!!!

Kevin: It's a chance in a lifetime.

Elaine: It's not even the real space centre.

Kevin: Similar.

Elaine:	How can Stuart Kennedy's 'Space kamp with a "K" off the A1' be anything like it!! I dread to think where he got these blue jump suits from and what's NISA?
Kevin:	It's supposed to be 'NASA' but he run out of A's.
Elaine:	Run out of A's!! [pause] And I also know the astronauts' helmets that we wore earlier, were not astronaut helmets.
Kevin:	Oh, now come on!!
Elaine:	Colanders!!
Kevin:	No need for that language!
Elaine:	Colanders, Kevin, the bowl you use in the kitchen.
Kevin:	Why do you think that?
Elaine:	[pulls out a strand of spaghetti from her hair, next line almost in tears] Spaghetti, Kevin, spaghetti! I spent the whole morning in an itchy blue jump suit and a colander on my head!!
Kevin:	Listen, babe, the first activity was good, wasn't it?
Elaine:	What, the landing and driving on Mars in full-motion simulators? As soon as it started shaking, Dave threw up on my shoes and Frank had a nosebleed. I ended up docking the space craft whilst covered in sick and blood! It was like a night at some sort of seedy nightclub. Oh, not forgetting Trevor sneezing into his colander.
Kevin:	He did ask for a tissue!
Elaine:	Yes, I did try to find one, but I couldn't remember which one of my 32 Velcro pockets I'd put it in.
Kevin:	He said it was because of the altitude.
Elaine:	Yes, he did have an attitude! [pause] and as for the simulator. Stuart's old caravan, with Micky pushing it from side to side!
Kevin:	Look, we're here now and we're halfway through. I loved that bag of sweets you brought along.

Elaine:	I just think it needed to be clearer, I thought the list was our favourite things. You love milky ways, mars bars and galaxy bars.
Kevin:	They were referring to planets, love. Planets.
Elaine:	I know that now.
Kevin:	You did sit down sharpish when Stuart said, 'Saturn, Uranus!'
Elaine:	Well you can talk! You were the one that said Pluto was Mickey's dog.
Kevin:	I just got confused.
Elaine:	And a dwarf planet is not called Dopey!! [*pause*] Then we had to make robots.
Kevin:	That was fun.
Elaine:	Toilet rolls, duct tape and stickers!!
Kevin:	Yours was lovely!
Elaine:	Oh why, Kevin, why?
Kevin:	Alright, so maybe it isn't quite how I imagined it!
Elaine:	And the food Kevin, the food.
Kevin:	Well it was proper space food, I think.
Elaine:	Dog biscuits Kevin, it tasted like dog biscuits.
Kevin:	Now, we did get treated to ice cream last night though, didn't we?
Elaine:	Yes, but eating upside down whilst swinging on ropes, didn't do it for me!!
Kevin:	Alright love, I understand. I just wanted to do something nice, in case I'm not here too much longer.
Elaine:	[*pause, close to tears*] Oh, Kevin is it the big 'C'?
Kevin:	I'm afraid so.
Elaine:	How long you got?
Kevin:	About three weeks.
Elaine:	Three weeks! What sort of cancer is it?
Kevin:	Cancer?

Elaine: You said the big 'C'.

Kevin: No, big Carl.

Elaine: So, what's the three weeks?

Kevin: Three weeks to pay him back for these tickets. I didn't have the money and I wanted to treat you.

Elaine: Oh, you daft sod, for a minute I thought you were a gonner! [*pause*] Come on.

Kevin: Where are we going?

Elaine: Space camp BBQ.

Kevin: I though the schedule said indoors, playing a game of 'The floor is Lava' in the galaxy tent.

Elaine: It did, but I persuaded everyone to meet outside.

Kevin: Why?

Elaine: Because Stuart's out there looking for aliens.

Kevin: Again? He does that every night. I can't see how that is worth watching.

Elaine: Let's just say, I gave him a few useful tips.

Kevin: Like what?

Elaine: Well, I told him that a spaceship runs on electricity and what with the storms coming in, he didn't want to get electrocuted. So, I came up with a way that would stop that happening.

Kevin: How's that then?

Elaine: Come and have a look. Have you ever seen a man with nothing on, but a rubber handled frying pan on his head?

Kevin: He hasn't, has he...?

Slimming for summer

Clare is at the front of the slimming class, Julie enters, she is 24, a bit more than curvy and looks like she doesn't want to be there.

Clare: Hello there!!! Please take a seat, don't be shy! Welcome to Lighter Life... You are...?

Julie: Julie.

Clare: Take a seat over there in the new member's corner. I do the talk for new members at the end.

Julie: I don't really know if...

Clare: Yes, if you just turn left behind the last row of chairs... Move in Beryl, only a bit now Beryl as you lost another 4 pounds this week [*clapping*]. Yes, that's it, don't worry we can put those chairs back in a line in a minute.

Julie: Maybe I should just...

Clare: Maybe turn that one sideways. That's it... Now, just behind the divider the one with pictures of Ryvita's and laughing cows. [*laughter is heard*] I heard that, Marge. Don't talk about Pat like that, it was her son's wedding!

Julie: I can always just...

Clare:	That's it, be with you shortly or tall-i.e., We don't judge here.
Julie:	Sorry?
Clare:	No need to be sorry, it's never too late. [*pause*] Alright everyone. So, Jayne will announce the raffle winner for the bowl of fruit, then if you can all just stack the chairs and, 'I hope to see less of you all next week'! [*walks over to Julie*]
	So...
Julie:	Julie Carter.
Clare:	So, Julie Carter, a warm welcome to 'Lighter than Life'. How did you hear about us?
Julie:	My mum. She used to come.
Clare:	She doesn't come any more, did she reach her target?
Julie:	Yes, she was doing it because she was going on holiday to Benidorm, with her boyfriend.
Clare:	So, she could wear her bikini in the sun? Fantastic!
Julie:	No, it was her first time flying and she wanted to be able to put the tray down when her lunch arrived.
Clare:	Was she successful?
Julie:	Her boyfriend dumped her, said she was too skinny, so she never even got to Benidorm.
Clare:	What a shame, a real achievement though in losing the weight.
Julie:	Suppose so.
Clare:	Anyway, let's talk about you, how much would you like to lose?
Julie:	Well. Really, I just wanted a boob reduction. I'm having a bit of trouble with this bra.
	I ordered it last Thursday, it came, but it must be the wrong size.
Clare:	Maybe you've just put on a tad of weight, nothing to worry about.

Julie:	Still think the boob job is a better solution.
Clare:	I promise you Julie, this is a much better solution!!
Julie:	I blame my mum's side of the family. I've got her body shape. Next year, I'm 25, it's all downhill then, knockers that I have to start tucking in my socks.
Clare:	What about if I told you. We can set you up on a plan to lose weight, reduce your boobs and be healthy. But...
Julie:	Yeah, that's also too big. Not in a good way either. Not a Kim Kardashian bum, or a J Lo.
Clare:	What I was going to say was... but... you need to be committed to change!
Julie:	My bum looks more like a squashed doughnut. I can't eat doughnuts on this diet, can I?
Clare:	We have many alternative sweet treats. I can show you our range of products at the end.
Julie:	Alright!
Clare:	Also, we have savoury alternatives. A Doner kebab for instance.
Julie:	I like kebabs.
Clare:	Yes, you use lettuce leaves instead of the pitta bread.
Julie:	Not a kebab then.
Clare:	Big Mac.
Julie:	I like Big Macs.
Clare:	Yes, you leave off the bun and have five percent or less mince with the salad and one ounce of light cheese.
Julie:	Not a Big Mac then.
Clare:	We do have to compromise if we want to reach our goals. Talk me through your daily eating plan.
Julie:	I'm only doing this because mum says, if I don't lose weight, I could have health issues.
Clare:	Sounds good advice.

Julie:	I told her, if she kept on, she'd have health issues… Then she brought out the big guns. Lose weight or she stops paying my phone bill. So here I am.
Clare:	Ok, so talk me through a typical 'Julie day.'
Julie:	I get up at 10, usually go to the toilet. I had a curry a couple of nights ago, so it's usually a bit of a burn. Then I have a fag…
Clare:	Not every part of the day, just the food parts.
Julie:	So, it's then usually eleven so I have a cup of tea and a couple of biscuits.
Clare:	Two isn't bad.
Julie:	Packets.
Clare:	Next?
Julie:	Then I have lunch, I'm quite healthy at lunch time.
Clare:	Glad to hear it.
Julie:	I have salad on my burger and an apple pie, followed by an assortment of fruit… in my doughnut. Later, just a snack. Box of Pringles. In the evening usually a pizza. I do get in my five a day then. I have four pieces of pineapple on my pizza, followed by chocolate orange.
Clare:	Oh dear, this is going to be harder than I thought. Any exercise?
Julie:	Yes.
Clare:	Fantastic!
Julie:	I have to walk to the chippie as mum won't let me borrow the car.
Clare:	I think, I will have to put you on the GREEN diet.
Julie:	What does that mean?
Clare:	You only eat foods that are green.
Julie:	There aren't any foods that are green.
Clare:	Of course, there are, broccoli, runner beans, cabbage, lettuce, cucumber.

Julie:	Just that!?
Clare:	The results will be incredible! Shall I sign you up for membership?
Julie:	I suppose so. Oh, I've got a coupon here in this magazine. Page 67, I think.
Clare:	Fantastic.
Julie:	Oh no, that's not the page. What's this... 'new chip shop opens this Thursday,' that's today! '1st 100 people in, get large Cod and medium chips for free'!!
Clare:	Julie, is that wise?
Julie:	No, you're right!
Clare:	Glad to hear it!
Julie:	It should be large Cod and large chips.
Clare:	But what about your health, what about this membership, what about your phone bill?
Julie:	That's alright, I can walk there! The money I save today I can pay for my own phone bill.
Clare:	But what about your green plan?
Julie:	Don't worry Clare, I'll have a pickled gherkin with it!

Sun, sea, and Ouzo

Millie and George reminisce about their recent time in Greece.

Millicent: So, we've just come back from our grand-daughter's wedding, beautiful it was.

George: Beautiful it was.

Millicent: She married a Greek. So, the wedding was on a beautiful Greek island.

George: Beautiful it was.

Millicent: When she first told us, we weren't sure what she was marrying.

George: On account of when she phoned us, she said she was marrying a lesbian.

Millicent: Well, we thought that's what she said. Turns out when we asked her who was she getting married to...

George: She thought we said, where was she getting married....

Millicent: Not a lesbian. But in Lesbos, it's a Greek Island.

George: Lesbos, not lesbian.

Millicent: Beautiful it was.

George: Beautiful it was.

Millicent: The journey was ok; we won't say any more about that. George doesn't like long journeys. But he's alright when he gets there.

George: I'm alright when I get there.

Millicent: The ceremony was beautiful.

George: Beautiful.

Millicent: Her fiancée/husband is called Darius Constantine Demetrius Angelopoulos.

George: I called him 'D'.

Millicent: Absolutely, beautiful he is, like a Greek actor...

George: Greek actor.

Millicent: George, do you remember when they asked us if we knew any Greek actors? You said John Travolta because you thought they said 'Grease'.

George: Telly Savalas.

Millicent: Was he in *Grease*?

George: No, he's Greek.

Millicent: Really?

George: Yeah.

Millicent: Well, I never knew that! Oh, and Nanna Mouskouri.

George: Moussaka, that was nice, wasn't it?

Millicent: Lovely. I had the tzatziki.

George: Bless you!!

Millicent: And the taramaladingdong.

George: Yes, the dancing was good.

Millicent: Later in the evening Darius's mother asked us if we would like a baklava. I mean it had got a bit chilly, but it certainly wasn't cold enough for a hat!

George: Cake was beautiful.

Millicent: Beautiful! So were the plates.

George: Shame they smashed them at the end.

Millicent: Anyway, it was all going perfectly until the disaster happened.

George: Disaster.

Millicent: Darius's brother Damen Constantine Demetrius Angelopoulos, turned up.

George: I call him 'D2'.

Millicent: So, Damen, was stinking of booze.

George: Stinking of booze.

Millicent: Apparently according to his great grandmother, Sophia. His wife Ophelia had thrown him out and chucked all his clothes outside the local taverna.

George: Outside the taverna.

Millicent: Apparently, he'd been having liaisons with Katerina from the 'Acropolis'. It's the restaurant near where they live.

George: Not the real Acropolis.

Millicent: We had a day trip to the real Acropolis, didn't we George? Beautiful.

George: Yeah. Be nice when it's finished.

Millicent: So anyway, Damen turned up at the wedding worse for wear. He made a scene!!

George: Made a scene.

Millicent: Been on the Ouzo all day, apparently...

George: Ouzo all day.

Millie: He kept crying into his gyro.

George: That's a kebab, not a benefit.

Millie: So, Damen, in his drunken state, knocks into the band, while they're playing a rendition of 'Zobra the Greek'. Broke his bazooka in half!!

George: The one on the mandolin, went straight in the pool.

Millicent: Anyway, Grandma Sophia threw Damen out, yelling in some sort of language.

George: It's all Greek to me!

Millicent: Then it all continued like nothing had happened.

George: Like nothing had happened. It reminded me of Clytemnestra, who plotted revenge for the killing of the couple's daughter, Iphigeneia, by Agamemnon himself.

[*Pause*]

Millicent: Did it?

September Heights – construction sites

Bert and Andrew are sitting at the side of a large construction site, while cranes move around them, other workers mix cement and give orders.

Bert: So, Danny, we've been working for about an hour, so it's… lunch time according to my reckoning.

Andrew: It's Andrew, actually.

Bert: Are you sure?

Andrew: Yes.

Bert: So, what do you think of your first week Andy?

Andrew: It's been alright, I suppose.

[*They open their lunch boxes, Bert's is white Tupperware, Andrew's is from John Lewis and has compartments*]

Bert: Cheese and pickle. All week she makes me cheese and pickle. I think I had this yesterday.

Andrew: Well, you would if you have had it all week.

Bert: No, I think this actual sandwich, I remember I didn't get time to finish it, I recognise the bite mark. What have you got?

Andrew: Salmon on rye, dijonaise and a little dill.

Bert: A little what?

Andrew: Dill.

Bert: Has your wife cut the crusts off.

Andrew: [*embarrassed*] Yes.

Bert: That won't last. How long have you been married?

Andrew: Two years.

Bert: Cheese and pickle this week, crab last week.

Andrew: Crab is nice.

Bert: Paste. [*pause*] The other week she tried me on some multi grain brown bread. Awful it was, I spent the whole day picking seeds out my teeth. I was trying to mix cement that afternoon, with a flock of pigeons, circling me. Pecked nearly to death!! [*pause*] That's my marriage!

Andrew: I'm sure she's just being caring.

Bert: Meat substitute she gave me! Meat substitute! I told her I'll have chips instead of a burger if I want a meat substitute.

Andrew: Do you think the foreman will give me next Wednesday off? [*pause*] We're trying for a baby.

Bert: Can't you be like everyone else and do it in the evening.

Andrew: No, it's an appointment to see a specialist, we are having a bit of trouble.

Bert: I only had to look at my Mrs and she got pregnant!

Andrew: Oh, you have children.

Bert: Yep, Mark, Spencer, Holland, and Barrett.

Andrew: Oh, easy to remember like the shops.

Bert: What shops? We go to the co-op. [*looks at Andrew*] Just a minute [*slightly lifts the hardhat*] Has your wife put your name in your hard hat?

Andrew: [*embarrassed*] Well, yes.

Bert: And your viz vest, oh Andy!!

Andrew: She's just trying to be supportive, that's all.

Bert: If you don't mind Andy, can I ask? Why construction? I don't mean to be rude, but you don't seem the type.

Andrew: Well, I'm actually, a writer.

Bert: Oh yeah, out of work, struggling. Think you're really good. Unfortunately, you tell me you have only ever had an article printed in the college newspaper. Everyone's a writer. Heard it all before. Decent job this, good wage, plenty of fresh air. [*pause*] What do you see when you look at these hands?

Andrew: Blisters and callouses?

Bert: A good day's work. Writers, they don't have hands like these. They have paper cuts. So, how did you find out about this place then, Jackie Collins?

Andrew: Well Trevor, is my uncle.

Bert: Big Trev? Security Trev, is your uncle?

Andrew: And with Miriam wanting a baby, I needed a good wage.

Bert: Oh, I see. Good luck to you I say. [*pause*] What sort of books do you write then.

Andrew: Mainly true stories, based on real characters. All their little idiosyncrasies.

Bert: Yeah, certainly a lot of idiots about. I don't think you'd get too much material on a building site though! [*he pours out a coffee and dips in a yorkie bar*] Swirl the coffee twice to the left, once to the right, followed by two dunks of my yorkie. Can't beat it!

Andrew: Takes all sorts.

Bert: You're not wrong there Andy. [*removes his hard hat to reveal a hair net*]

Pumpkin pie and apple cider

Two mates in the pub. Trevor is sitting, Stewpot arrives, they stand at the bar.

Trev: Alright Stewpot.

Stewpot: Yeah, you?

Trev: I'm in the doghouse again. It's a wonder I haven't got a basket and a bowl.

Stewpot: What you been up to now?

Trev: Women, I don't understand them!

Stewpot: I gave up understanding them after I split from Tracy. I went over to the other side.

Trev: You mean you're.

Stewpot: No, the other side of the estate. The bit that overlooks the industrial park, rather than the fishmongers. Better smell.

Trev: Have you tried this Halloween 'apple cider'? It's not bad. I also got the last slice of pumpkin pie. I don't usually eat fruit.

Stewpot: Pumpkin is a vegetable.

Trev: Is it? Well, there you go, Michelle would be pleased, she loves fruit and veg. That is, if she was talking to me.

Stewpot: So, what did you do?

Trev: Well firstly, she said I don't listen to anything she says.

Stewpot: So, what was she saying?

Trev: No, idea! [pause] Last night she said I hadn't noticed the change.

I said, 'what change?' Apparently, she'd cut her hair from shoulder length to short and dyed it a different colour. I would have noticed at some point!

Stewpot: Is that why she's not talking to you?

Trev: No, she said I don't do any jobs.

Stewpot: Like what?

Trev: Apparently, she asked me a few months ago to clear out the junk in the shed. I told her, to write it down. Write down what she needs me to do.

Stewpot: Did she?

Trev: Apparently. She wrote a list of everything in there, what to keep and what to throw.

Stewpot: Did you?

Trev: No, she put the list in the shed. I'm not going in there it's full of junk.

Stewpot: So that's what did it.

Trev: No. She said it wasn't the shed. It wasn't the not listening and it wasn't the romantic meal.

Stewpot: Romantic meal?

Trev: She asked me to buy one. One of them Marks Dine from home meal and a bottle of bubbly. Also, to run a hot bath for her full of bubbles.

Stewpot: Sounds nice.

Trev: Well, only got caught up with 'one eyed Ian' watching the match. When I looked at my watch. I had half an hour to buy it, cook it and present it.

Stewpot: So, what did you do?

Trev: Stopped off at the kebab shop, Two Doners, Two bottles of beer. Bought a bottle of chilli sauce and thought, that's it! Job done.

Stewpot: Did you get back in time?

Trev: Yes, even made chilli sauce hearts on the side and took the lid off the beers.

Stewpot:	What about the bath?
Trev:	Well, that's it. I didn't have enough time for that. I just filled up the sink and put a new Palmolive soap by the side.
Stewpot:	Nice. Job done. [*pause*] What did she say?
Trev:	Well, she wasn't best pleased. I tried really hard to smooth it over. I even complimented her and said she didn't look dirty at all so probably didn't need a bath.
Stewpot:	So that's what did it.
Trev:	No.
Stewpot:	So, what then?
Trev:	She suggested going to Yvonne's Halloween party and maybe we should go as a couple. 'A couple of what?' I said.
Stewpot:	Go on.
Trev:	Then she said *Titanic*.
Stewpot:	Nice one, Jack and Rose.
Trev:	Now, I know that. I've never seen the film, so I said. Perfect, you can wear that black and white striped dress that makes you look big, and I will wear all white and go as an iceberg.
	So that's why I'm in the doghouse.

Here come the fireworks

Clive is sitting on a bench in the park. Jill enters.

Jill: Mind if I sit here? My feet are killing me!

Clive: Well, I...

          [Jill *sits anyway*]

Jill: I was supposed to go over to my friend Sophie's house. I was on my way, but then she called me. 'Jill,' she said 'my boyfriend has come back early from his business trip, so can we re-schedule? [*pause*] It was only going to be Netflix and a takeaway, so you see I didn't put the right shoes on for an outdoor activity. But I said to myself, 'Jill, don't turn back and go home, go over to the firework display, get some fresh air in your lungs, Jill'.

Clive: I am actually waiting for someone; she should be here any minute.

Jill: Oh, of course, what does she look like? I'll keep an eye out for her.

Clive: Well, I don't actually know...

Jill: Oh, it's a blind date. Have you got a photo?

Clive: No, it's an all-inclusive website.

Jill: That just means you haven't got much choice. Like when I go to the corner shop late at night and I end up with custard creams rather than Maryland cookies. [*pause*] So, what is your type?

Clive: I don't have a type.

Jill: Everyone has a type.

Clive: I don't. Maybe... a sense of humour.

Jill:	So, if she turns up covered in pimples, greasy hair, and bad breath, but can tell a good knock knock joke, you're happy. Everyone has a type. Maybe the wrong type, but a type. I always go for the wrong type. I can't seem to help it. First there was Roy, he spent all his time in the pub, every date we had was in the pub. Arranged a surprise party for me... in the pub. Got a job... in the pub. Literally, we never went anywhere else.
Clive:	Oh... If you don't mind, I...
Jill:	Then there was Mike, he was cool. Had a motorbike. I rode on the back once. One time we hit this bump in the road. I remember hearing him say...'My love, my love. I can't live without you'!
Clive:	Well, that sounds thoughtful.
Jill:	He was talking to the bike!!! Then there was Steve... he... Oh my god, that's him over there with that girl. OMG. [*starts laughing really loudly*] Oh, you're SOOO funny! Harry.
Clive:	It's Clive. [Jill *grabs* Clive *by the ears and gives him a big smacker, muffled speech*] Did he see us?
Clive:	I don't know!! [*he tries to break away but the buttons on their tops are caught together*]
	I can't seem to...
Jill:	Alright you can let me go.
Clive:	I can't, I'm...
Jill:	You can't be in love with me already, I mean...
Clive:	I can't because, our buttons are attached!
Jill:	Oh yes! Just a sec. There we go.
Clive:	Look... Jill...
Jill:	How do you know my name?
Clive:	You said it earlier when you did your monologue about your shoes.

Jill: Is it hot out here? I'm really hot. Is it hot out here?

Clive: No, it's November.

Jill: [*removing items*] Phew!! Must be those antibiotics I'm taking for my rash; it said the side effects could be hot sweats. They weren't kidding [*takes the red hand-kerchief,* Clive *has in his top pocket*]

Goodness, it's like a tropical forest. Ow! was that a mosquito? Ow!

Clive: Can I have my handkerchief back please.

Jill: Oh yes sorrym [*there is now a large pile of clothes between them,* Jill *is just in a t-shirt now*] That's it, isn't it? That's how she knows you are her date, by the red scarf. Oh, that's brilliant. What time are the fireworks starting?

Clive: Should be any minute now.

Jill: Do you live around here... erm...?

Clive: Clive.

Jill: I had a dog called Clive once, he looked a bit like you, actually.

Clive: I beg your pardon?

Jill: I just meant kind eyes that's all.

Clive: Oh, I see.

Jill: Do you think you've been stood up?

Clive: [*irritated*] I don't know.

Jill: My aunt's single. Now, she has got a good sense of humour. And that isn't code for ugly.

Shall I give you her number? She won't mind.

Clive: No, it's fine. [*phone bleeps*] Oh it's her... [*reading*] 'Sorry, I have gone home. You looked very cosy on the bench with your blonde friend!'

Jill: Me with you? As if... [*pause*] Shame, she obviously did have a sense of humour!! [*starts to put all her layers back on*]

Clive:	Maybe I will take your aunt's number.
Jill:	That's the spirit. [*looks at her phone*] It's... Oh it's Sophie, she's what? trying to throw her boyfriend out! She found out he wasn't on a business trip at all. He was staying with his secretary!! Oh dear, she wants me to go around there, straight away.
Clive:	But what about the fireworks?
Jill:	They'll be plenty of fireworks round Sophie's!
Clive:	Well, see you then.
Jill:	[*still looking at her phone*] Yeah, nice to have met you. Oh, my aunt, you wanted her number. Now, what did I put it under? Oh, I know! You can just meet her face to face. She owns the tattoo parlour in the high street. 'Get your tats out'. She's great!!
Clive:	Oh, ok then.
Jill:	See you then. Me and you!! That's hilarious!! [*laughs*] Enjoy the fireworks. [*into the phone, as she leaves*] I'm coming Sophie!! I can't wait to tell you the story of the bloke I met in the park.
	[*The sound of fireworks is heard;* Clive *looks up in the air and enjoys the show*]

Christmas Bingo

Rita is seated, Liz has entered the bingo hall.

Rita: Cooeee, Liz, oh she can't hear me she's got her reindeer ear muffs on. [*waves her hands in the air*] Cooeee, Liz. Oh, she's turned left, Cooeee Liz, she can hear me, her ears pricked up. She just can't see me. Cooeee, Liz. Oh, some one's pointing at me, yes, she's waving, oh, here she comes.

Liz: You won't believe the morning I've had! I was early for the bus, so I treated myself to a Gregg's sausage roll. Well... you won't believe it!!

Rita: What?

Liz: No sausage in it!!

Rita: No!!

Liz: So, I went back. I said there's no sausage in this roll, just pastry!

'No sausage in this roll, just pastry?' he said, as if I was mad. Then he said, 'Are you sure you haven't eaten the sausage?' I mean, I know I'm getting old, but I wouldn't have forgotten that I'd eaten the sausage!!

Rita: What did he say?

Liz: Said I could have another free of charge, but I'd have to wait for another batch, at least 20 minutes!! I'll have something else I said. 'Nice baps', he said!! I ignored him; he was young enough to be my grandson. They'd run out of the chocolate yule log. So, I settled on a steak slice and a yum yum.

Rita: Nice.

Liz: Trouble is I missed the bus. I was covered in flaky pastry. Halfway through my yum yum by the time I got the next one.

Rita: Never mind. They're starting another game in five minutes, full house is £250 and a deluxe Christmas pudding. Have you got your lucky dabber?

Liz: Then, I missed the stop, had to walk back. What a morning!!

Rita: Oh, I think that was the first number. Two fat ladies...

Liz: I'm still covered in flaky pastry. Two fat ladies!! Sounds like us, Rita. [*gets dabber*] Ok 88!! Got that!

Rita: Lucky seven!

Liz: That's the bus I got on. I didn't feel very lucky.

Rita: Sshh!

Liz: 38!

Rita: Is that was he said? Is that the next number?

Liz: No, that's the bus I should have got on. [*pause*] Now me dabbers not working? What did he say?

Rita: 44, 18 and 5.

Liz: I'll use this pencil.

Rita: Sshh, I'm trying to hear.

Liz: Talking of hearing. I've got my doctor's appointment, next Wednesday, get my ears syringed.

Rita: Number one, Kelly's eye.

Liz: No, my eyes are alright, it's just so dark in here.

Rita:	22, 63, 10.
Liz:	Got that, haven't got that one, got that. Not bad...
Rita:	SSh!!
Liz:	Have you got a cold, I've got a tissue in my bag somewhere, I had it around my steak slice, but I can fold it.
Rita:	Full house?!! Oh, it's Ivy. She wins every time.
Liz:	Oh, what a shame, you were doing so well. How about a mince pie and a glass of mulled wine? We can catch up. I haven't spoken to you since last Tuesday's Christmas scrabble. Speaking of Christmas. Did I tell you about the Christmas dinner I had in the Wetherspoons?
	[*both getting up*]
Rita:	What, no turkey?
Liz:	No, don't be silly, no crackers.
Rita:	Cream crackers?
Liz:	No, Christmas crackers, honestly Rita, you're not with it today, are you? Remind me to go in Tesco's on the way home. I need to take back the scarf, Maude bought me it last Christmas. It's far too flashy!!
Rita:	You won't get a refund, a year later.
Liz:	Oh no. I know that I want to get a large envelope so I can send it to her, as a Christmas present.
Rita:	Oh!
Liz:	She won't remember, she's getting old. And I'll tell you one thing...
Rita:	What?
Liz:	She'll definitely like it. After all... she picked it, didn't she?
Rita:	I suppose so.
Liz:	Don't buy me anything, will you?
Rita:	I already did.

Liz: Oh, alright. Maybe you want the scarf then? It would suit you!!

[*wander off, arm in arm*]